HUNGARIAN DESSERT BOOK

© ALL RIGHTS RESERVED.
Without limiting the rights under copyright reserved above, no part of this publication may be reproduced, stored in or introduced into a retrieval system, or transmitted, in any form or by any means (electronic, mechanical, photocopying, recording or otherwise), without the prior written permission of the copyright owner and the above publisher of the book. The content of the book is subject to alteration without notice.

PUBLISHED BY BOOOK PUBLISHING HUNGARY 2017
Web: www.boook.hu | Facebook: www.facebook.hu/Boook | Email: info@boook.hu

Editor: **Tamás Bereznay**
Art direction and graphic design: **Hajnal Földi**
Cover painting: **Lászlóné Romsics**
Publisher: **Péter Széplaki**

Food photography: **Imre Körmendi**
Food styling: **Ágnes Kapolka**
Translation and culinary supervisor: **Sue Tolson**
Proofreader: **Robert Smyth**

Printed in Reálszisztéma Dabas Printing House, 2017
ISBN 978-615-5417-7-7
Hungarian Dessert Book, Boook Publishing

TAMÁS BEREZNAY
HUNGARIAN DESSERT BOOK

CONTENTS

CAKES
- 16 Pear Gateau
- 19 Rich chocolate cake
- 20 Granny's walnut cake
- 23 Eszterházy cake
- 24 Stefánia cake
- 27 Poppy seed cake
- 28 Five jam cake
- 31 Dobos cake
- 35 Blueberry tart
- 36 Cinnamon cake
- 39 Layered pancakes

SAVOURY DESSERTS
- 44 Caraway bread rolls
- 47 Cabbage turnovers
- 48 Crackling scones
- 51 Potato scones

STRUDELS
- 57 Sour cherry strudels
- 58 Sour cherry and poppy seed strudel
- 61 Apple strudel
- 62 Chocolate strudel
- 65 Chesnut strudel

HOT DESSERTS
- 71 Walnut pancake
- 72 Noodle and curd cheese cake with berries
- 75 Pancakes stuffed with plum jam and brandy
- 79 Rice soufflé
- 80 Curd cheese dumplings
- 83 Honey- and jam-filled apple
- 84 Apple and meringue bread and butter pudding
- 87 Curd cheese dumpling soufflé
- 88 Curd cheese stuffed rolls
- 91 Plum jam and poppy seed vermicelli
- 92 Golden walnut dumplings
- 95 Baked plum jam doughnuts
- 96 Doughnuts
- 99 Poppy seed bread pudding
- 100 Emperor's crumbs
- 103 Pasta pockets filled with plum jam
- 104 Sour cherry purses
- 104 Prune and marzipan fritters
- 108 Jam-filled crescent roll fritters
- 111 Chimney cake
- 112 Gundel pancake
- 114 Buns with cocoa (cinnamon, plum jam)

MISCELLANEOUS
- 120 Plum tart
- 123 Raspberry and cream sponge roll
- 124 Semolina cream with prunes
- 127 Quince cheese
- 128 Floating islands
- 131 Cream slices
- 132 Frosted slices
- 135 Zserbó sliced
- 136 Poppy seed cup cake
- 139 Honey cream slices
- 140 Non plus ultra
- 143 Apple and cream slices
- 144 Pear cake with almonds
- 147 Somló trifle
- 149 Linzer jam sandwich biscuits
- 150 Flódni jewish cake
- 153 Coconut balls
- 154 Sour cherry pie
- 157 Walnut crescents
- 158 Fried curd cheese doughnut
- 161 Chestnut purée
- 162 Curd cheese parcels
- 165 Sweet twisted fritters
- 167 Dill and curd cheese pie
- 168 Chocolate and walnut cake
- 171 Plaited brioche

INTRODUCTION

Everyone loves cakes and sweet things, and the Hungarians are no exception to this, in fact I would say that the nation as a whole has a sweeter tooth than most. The streets of Hungary's towns and cities are lined with cafés and cake shops. Even the smallest of towns will boast at least one cake shop. The capital, Budapest, like Vienna, is renowned for its coffeehouses, where the literary elite used to congregate in the past, regaling each other with their works, or simply taking advantage of the warmth and coffee to read and write, and now locals and tourists alike will sit down for a coffee and a slice of cake from the vast array behind the glass counters. Coffeehouse favourites such as strudel, Dobos cake, chestnut purée, and Eszterházy cake are lined up behind the glass to tempt the hungry, or once you glimpse them, the even not so hungry, to partake in their sweet delights, along with more innovative modern creations in some cases.

However, it is not only in coffeehouses and cafés that Hungarians enjoy cakes and other sweet delicacies. Most families have at least one accomplished baker, and all parties and other festivities will involve a variety of baked goods, both sweet and savoury, for the delectation of the family and other visitors. Indeed, Hungarians enjoy sweet things so much that the focal part of a meal, the main course so to say, may well be something sweet. Especially when visiting relatives of friends in the countryside, I discovered it was often the case that the meal consisted of some soup followed by something sweet. Milk loaf, pasta with poppy seeds or walnuts and plenty of sugar, pancakes in all shapes and forms, doughnuts or maybe apricot or curd cheese dumplings. Then, when you sat down to chat with a coffee, you would be plied further with biscuits, scones and cake, too. One thing is certain; you'll never leave Hungary having lost weight!

There is a range of ingredients that find particular favour with the nation in sweets and desserts, some of which are widespread elsewhere, like honey, sour cream, chocolate, jam and fruit, especially plums, apricots and sour cherries, and some of which are perhaps used more commonly in this part of the world, such as curd cheese, poppy seeds, walnuts and chestnut purée. *Túró*, a kind of curd cheese, is popular in both savoury and sweet dishes and finds its way into many of the recipes in this book. It is something quite particular to Hungary, so if you can't find it, you could perhaps substitute it with ricotta or German-style quark. It is often translated as cottage cheese, but it is in fact nothing like what we call cottage cheese.

Poppy seeds, which elsewhere would be relegated to a sprinkling on top of a bread roll, are a key ingredient in all sorts of sweet treats, including strudel and *flódni*. Walnuts, generally ground, end up in many cakes and biscuits as well as the delicious Gundel pancake. Chestnuts, which are often only enjoyed elsewhere at Christmas time, also play a role in the creation of sweet things, generally in the form of chestnut purée, which you can buy in blocks at the supermarket. A particular favourite of mine is simple chestnut purée and cream on offer in autumn and winter in coffee houses, but chestnut purée also forms the basis of some delicious cakes and strudel, too.

Tamás shows us how to make both tasty homely family treats and desserts as well as how to attempt the more sophisticated creations on display in the coffeehouses. Whatever your taste in sweet things, you're sure to find something to tempt you to start creating, cooking and baking. Enjoy.

Sue Tolson, *Managing Editor of WineSofa, online wine and food adventures in Central and Eastern Europe*

CAKES

PEAR GATEAU (KÖRTETORTA)

INGREDIENTS

FOR THE CAKE MIXTURE
7 eggs
200g sugar
100ml rum
zest of one lemon
150g ground walnuts
150g plain flour
½ tsp baking powder
½ tsp cloves
½ tsp ground cinnamon
150g apricot jam
pinch of salt

FOR THE FILLING
1 kg pears
100g honey
1 tsp cinnamon
150ml water
25g custard powder
1 tsp gelatine

FOR THE CREAM
400ml double cream
50ml water
1 tsp gelatine
150g icing sugar

Mix the egg yolks together with half the sugar, half the rum and the lemon zest in a bain-marie. Use a large enough pan to put the bowl in, bring the water to the boil, then simmer while gently whisking and cooking the ingredients to a thick cream. In another bowl, beat the egg whites with the remaining sugar and a pinch of salt until stiff peaks form. Mix the walnuts with the flour, baking powder, cinnamon and cloves. Now mix the beaten egg whites into the egg yolks and then gradually fold in the dry walnut mixture, too. Finally, spoon the mixture into a buttered and floured 30x25cm baking tray. Bake in a preheated 160°C oven for 30-35 minutes. Remove from the oven and leave to cool. Turn out onto a floured board and cut into three pieces. Cut the pears for the filling into cubes. Caramelise the honey, then add the pears and season with cinnamon. Stew the fruit, stirring constantly. Meanwhile, bring the custard powder to the boil with 100ml of water and add to the stewed pears. Mix the gelatine with 50ml of lukewarm water and add to the filling mixture. Whip the cream until thick. Now assemble the gateau. Spread the first layer of cake with half the apricot jam mixed with the remaining rum and spoon on the pear filling. Place the next layer on top and spread this with jam too, followed by the cream. Cover this with the final layer of cake and leave to chill in the fridge for at least 12 hours before serving.

RICH CHOCOLATE CAKE (RIGÓ JANCSI)

INGREDIENTS

FOR THE CAKE
6 eggs
160g sugar
130g plain flour
40g cocoa powder
100g melted butter

FOR THE CREAM
375g semi-bitter chocolate
50ml oil
600ml double cream

FOR THE FILLING
apricot jam

FOR THE TOPPING
chocolate couverture
½ tsp oil

Beat the eggs and sugar in a bain-marie. Remove from the heat before it begins to boil and continue to beat until thick and stiff. Gradually fold in the cocoa powder and flour a spoon at a time and then add the melted butter.
Spoon the mixture into a buttered and floured cake tin and bake in a preheated oven at 180°C for 35 minutes. Leave to cool, then halve the sponge horizontally and spread one of the cut sides with jam.
To make the cream, melt the chocolate and oil in a bain-marie. Beat the thoroughly chilled cream until thick and then add it to the melted chocolate. Put the sponge cake spread with jam back into the cake tin, jam side up, spread over the chocolate cream and top with the other half of the cake.
Melt the chocolate couverture with a little oil and coat the top of the cake with it. Chill for 6-7 hours in the fridge before serving.

GRANNY'S WALNUT CAKE
(NAGYIKÁM DIÓTORTÁJA)

INGREDIENTS

FOR THE CAKE
80g ground walnuts
80g icing sugar
7 eggs
1 tbsp breadcrumbs

FOR THE FILLING
80g walnuts
120g sugar
100ml water
60g butter

To make the cake batter, mix the walnuts, icing sugar and egg yolks together. Beat for a long time, even half an hour, so that it amalgamates well. Whisk the egg whites until stiff peaks form and fold in the breadcrumbs and the walnut mixture. Divide the batter into two and pour into cake tins. Bake both at 180°C for 15 minutes.
For the filling, heat the walnuts and sugar in the water. Then remove from the heat and mix in the butter. Keep beating until the cream cools down completely. Spread three-quarters of the cream onto one of the cake halves, then put the other half on top and spread the remaining cream onto the sides and top of the cake. Decorate with walnuts.

ESZTERHÁZY CAKE (ESZTERHÁZY TORTA)

INGREDIENTS

FOR THE CAKE
10 egg whites
350g granulated sugar
300g ground walnuts
50g plain flour
50g cake or breadcrumbs

FOR THE CREAM
20g custard powder
250ml milk
40g granulated sugar
80g walnuts
100ml cream
20g icing sugar
2cl cognac

FOR DECORATION
half an egg white
300g icing sugar
50g melted plain chocolate
100g ground walnuts

Beat the egg whites and the granulated sugar until they form stiff peaks. Carefully fold in the walnuts, flour and breadcrumb mixture. Preheat the oven to 180°C and bake six thin cake sheets on a greased, floured baking sheet (approx. 24cm in diameter) for about 6-8 minutes. Make a thick custard from the custard powder, sugar and milk, and allow to cool while stirring continuously. Whisk the cream and icing sugar until thick and add it to the custard, along with the walnuts and the cognac. Whisk until smooth. Spread cream onto each sheet and stack on each other, leaving the top bare. Beat half an egg white together with 300g icing sugar, then cover the whole cake with the mixture. Decorate the top with melted chocolate and the sides with ground walnuts.

STEFÁNIA CAKE (STEFÁNIA TORTA)

INGREDIENTS

FOR THE CAKE
6 eggs
120g flour
120g icing sugar
35g butter
pinch of salt

FOR THE FILLING
5 eggs
200g icing sugar
250g butter
200g chocolate
20g cocoa powder

Whisk the egg yolks and sugar together until white and creamy. Beat the egg whites until thick peaks form and fold into the yolks in three stages. Finally, add the pinch of salt and the melted butter. Spread the mixture into six 22cm cake tins and bake at 180°C for 12-14 minutes until golden brown.

Beat the eggs in a mixing bowl, add the sugar and heat in a bain-marie until it just starts to come to the boil. Then beat in a food processor as it cools down. Melt the chocolate in a bain-marie, remove from the heat and mix with the softened butter. Then mix the chocolate with the egg mixture and add the sifted cocoa powder.

Spread the cooled cream thinly on the first sponge sheet, add the next layer and so on to make a layer cake. Spread the top and sides with the remaining cream and sprinkle generously with cocoa powder.

POPPY SEED CAKE (MENNYEI MÁKTORTA)

INGREDIENTS

100g ground poppy seeds
400ml sour cream
3 tsp gelatine
100g sugar
1 sachet of vanilla sugar
200ml cream
100g cranberries or other red berries
6 gingerbread biscuits

Mix 100ml of sour cream with the gelatine and then heat until you obtain a homogenous mixture.
Pour into a mixing bowl and then add the sugar, vanilla sugar and the remaining sour cream.
Mix in the gingerbread broken into small pieces and the whipped cream.
Carefully mix in the cranberries, which you can of course substitute with sour cherries, redcurrants or other fruit, or if you don't actually have any fruit at home, then you can even leave out the fruit (in this case, after you pour the batter into the mould, you can add some jam to the cake).
Pour the mixture into a loaf tin lined with foil and cool for at least six hours in the fridge.

FIVE JAM CAKE (ÖTLEKVÁROS TORTA)

INGREDIENTS

300g margarine
300g icing sugar
300g ground walnuts
300g plain flour
3 whole eggs
½ tsp ground cloves
grated zest of 1 lemon
150g each of 5 flavours of jam

Mix all the cake ingredients together thoroughly, with the exception of the jam, and then chill for about half an hour in the fridge. Remove from the fridge and divide into six equal parts. Roll each part out into a circle and bake each sheet separately in a 170°C oven. Then spread each sheet with a different flavour jam, stack on top of each other, and dust the top with icing sugar.
If you only have two or three flavours of jam at home, your cake will still be delicious. This time I used orange marmalade, apricot, plum, strawberry and blueberry jam. The cake keeps well in the fridge, so you can make it up to five or six days before serving. The flavours will integrate better like this, too.

DOBOS CAKE (DOBOS TORTA)

INGREDIENTS

FOR THE CAKE
6 eggs
120g flour
120g icing sugar
35g butter
pinch of salt

FOR THE FILLING
5 eggs
200g icing sugar
250g butter
200g chocolate
20g cocoa powder

FOR THE CARAMEL
200g sugar cubes

Beat the egg yolks with the sugar until light and fluffy. Beat the egg whites until stiff and fold into the egg yolks in three stages. Finally, add the pinch of salt and the melted butter. Spread the mixture into six 22cm cake tins and bake at 180°C for 12-14 minutes until golden brown. Set the best sponge sheet aside for the top of the cake.
Put the sugar into a saucepan and caramelise without stirring. Lay the top sponge sheet onto a wire rack. Put some greaseproof paper underneath it so that you avoid dripping sugar all over the table. Pour the sugar over the sponge and cut into 12 slices with an oily knife before the caramel sets completely. Beat the eggs in a mixing bowl, add the sugar and heat in a bain-marie until it just starts to come to the boil. Then beat in a food processor as it cools down. Melt the chocolate in a bain-marie, remove from the heat and mix with the softened butter. Then mix the chocolate with the egg mixture and add the sifted cocoa powder. Spread the cooled cream thinly on the first sponge sheet, add the next layer and so on to make a layer cake. Spread the top and sides of the cake with the remaining cream and pipe on 12 small star-shaped balls. Press the caramel slices on top of these.

PUNCH CAKE (PUNCSTORTA)

INGREDIENTS

FOR THE CAKE:
12 eggs
12 tbsp flour
12 tbsp icing sugar
1 sachet of baking powder
pinch of salt

FOR THE FILLING:
2 tbsp raspberry jam
100ml water
100ml raspberry syrup
2 tbsp rum
juice of 1 orange and 1 lemon
100g sugar

FOR THE ICING:
200g icing sugar
few drops of lemon juice
100ml raspberry syrup
1 egg white
100ml apricot jam

Beat the egg yolks and sugar until creamy and then add the stiffly beaten egg whites and a pinch of salt. Then gradually fold in the flour mixed with the baking powder. Finally divide into two buttered and floured cake tins and bake at 180°C for 20-25 minutes.
Cut one of the cakes in half – this will form the top and bottom of the cake. Cut the other sponge into small cubes. Make a syrup by heating the water, raspberry jam, raspberry syrup, rum, sugar, and orange and lemon juice together. Drizzle over the sponge cubes and mix thoroughly.
Brush the cut sides of the cake sheets with the apricot jam.
Place one of them back in the cake tin, spread with the filling and cover with the other sheet of cake. Press down gently and chill for at least six hours in the fridge.
Meanwhile, prepare the icing. Whisk the ingredients together until smooth, then warm slightly in a bain-marie to make it easier to spread.
Remove the cake from the tin and spread the top and the sides with the icing. Let it set before cutting into slices.

BLUEBERRY TART (ÁFONYATORTA)

INGREDIENTS

FOR THE PASTRY
300g plain flour
200g butter
100g icing sugar
1 egg yolk
1-2 tsp sour cream
grated lemon zest
1 tsp vanilla sugar
pinch of baking powder
pinch of salt

FOR THE FILLING
5 egg yolks
300ml cream
1 tsp vanilla essence
150g granulated sugar
500g blueberries

Mix the flour with the icing sugar and then rub in the cold butter. Add a pinch of salt, the vanilla sugar, baking powder and grated lemon zest. Then knead in the egg yolk and enough sour cream to get a kneadable pastry.
Leave to rest in the fridge for an hour before using. Line a 25cm diameter flan dish with the pastry, prick with a fork and bake in a 170°C oven for 15 minutes. Tip: use as cold flour as possible to make the pastry and work quickly so that the pastry does not warm up from the heat of your hands. Always use fine plain flour.
Roll out the pastry and line a fluted flan dish with it. Bake in a preheated oven at 180°C for 10 minutes until golden brown.
Beat the eggs, cream, sugar and vanilla essence together until smooth. Pour the mixture into the pre-baked pastry case and sprinkle over the blueberries. Bake for 40 minutes in a 160°C oven.

CINNAMON CAKE (FAHÉJTORTA)

INGREDIENTS

FOR THE PASTRY
150g plain flour
100g butter
50g icing sugar
1 sachet of vanilla sugar
1 egg yolk
grated lemon zest
pinch of salt

FOR THE FILLING
3 eggs
150g granulated sugar
125ml cream
125ml milk
pinch of salt
1 tsp ground cinnamon
1 sachet of baking powder
200g ground almonds
4 gingerbread biscuits, crumbled
½ tsp candied lemon peel, finely chopped

First of all, make the pastry. Mix the flour with the icing sugar, vanilla sugar and a pinch of salt, then rub in the cold butter and add the grated lemon zest and the egg yolk.
Leave the pastry to rest in a cool place for half an hour, then line a fluted cake tin with it and bake for 15 minutes in a 180°C oven. Beat the eggs and sugar for the filling together until light and fluffy. Add the milk, cream, salt and cinnamon.
Finally, gradually fold in the gingerbread crumbs, almonds and lemon zest. Pour the mixture into the pastry case and bake for a further 45 minutes.

LAYERED PANCAKES
(CSÚSZTATOTT PALACSINTA)

INGREDIENTS

200ml milk
200ml cream
7 eggs
110g sugar
40g vanilla sugar
200g flour
pinch of salt
grated lemon and orange zest
oil or butter for frying

FOR THE FILLING
200g plain chocolate
100g ground walnuts
80g granulated sugar
½ tsp ground cinnamon

FOR THE COATING:
80g plain chocolate
50ml cream

Separate the eggs and beat the yolks with the sugar and vanilla sugar until light and fluffy. Add the milk, cream, salt, grated lemon and orange zest, and the flour. Finally beat the egg whites until stiff and loosen the batter with this.
Mix the ground walnuts with the cinnamon and sugar.
Fry thick pancakes in butter over a low heat. Place one on a plate, grate some chocolate over it and sprinkle it with the walnut mixture. Add another pancake, sprinkle it with more grated chocolate and walnuts. Repeat the process until you run out of pancakes.
Melt the remaining chocolate with the cream and coat the whole pancake cake with it.

SAVOURY DESSERTS

CARAWAY BREAD ROLLS (KÖMÉNYES KIFLI)

INGREDIENTS (MAKES 20 PIECES)

300g potatoes, cooked and mashed
3 egg yolks
350g flour
20g fresh yeast
100ml milk
1 tbsp of caraway seeds
50g butter
salt

Mix the potatoes with two egg yolks, salt, the milk, the flour and the crumbled yeast. Knead well on a floured surface for 5-10 minutes. Cover with a kitchen towel and let it rise for 20 minutes. Halve the dough and roll each piece out into 3mm-thick pieces. Cut each piece into 12 equal slices (just like a cake). With your hands, form bread rolls by rolling each piece up tightly, starting on the wide side and rolling toward the point. Place the rolls on a greased tray, brush with a lightly beaten egg yolk and sprinkle with caraway seeds. Butter a big oven pan, put the bread rolls on it and bake until golden brown in an oven at 180°C.

CABBAGE TURNOVERS (KÁPOSZTÁS HASÉ)

INGREDIENTS

500g puff pastry

FOR THE FILLING:
150g grated white cabbage
100g granulated sugar
salt
black pepper
100ml sunflower oil
1 egg yolk for glazing

Caramelise the sugar in the oil and add the grated cabbage. Season with a little salt and braise until golden brown, stirring constantly. Then add plenty of black pepper and, if necessary, a little more salt. Leave to cool.
Roll the pastry out thinly and cut it into 10x10 rectangles. Put two teaspoons of filling in the centre of each, fold in half and press the edges together. Brush the tops with the egg yolk mixed with a tablespoon of water.
Lay in a baking tray and bake for 20 minutes at 195°C.

CRACKLING SCONES (TEPERTŐS POGI)

INGREDIENTS

600g flour + 100-200g for folding
200g butter
300g mashed potatoes, boiled in their skins
27g sachets of dried yeast
40g salt
30g icing sugar
3 egg yolks
50ml milk
400g ground pork crackling
salt, pepper
1-2 egg yolks

Add the flour, potatoes, salt, yeast and icing sugar to a deep mixing bowl. Mix these dry ingredients together. Lightly beat the egg yolks and mix with the lukewarm milk. Melt the butter and add to the egg and milk mixture together with the flour mix. Knead thoroughly, either by hand or using a food processor. Sprinkle the top with flour, cover with a tea towel and leave to rise in a warm place for 40 minutes.
Then cover it with plenty of flour and roll out by hand into a rectangle approximately 70x40cm in size. Sprinkle the top with crackling pieces, and season with salt and pepper. Afterwards, fold both sides inward and then the upper and lower half into the middle. Press the whole dough together a little, turn it over, sprinkle with flour and leave to rest for 20 minutes.
Roll out the dough again, repeat the folding process and leave to rise. Repeat this four times for 20 minutes.
Finally, roll out to a thickness of 2cm with a rolling pin. Slash the top and cut out medium-sized scones. Place the scones on a baking sheet, brush with beaten egg yolk and bake in a 190°C oven for 30 minutes until golden brown.

POTATO SCONES (KRUMPLIS POGÁCSA)

INGREDIENTS (MAKES 25-30)

35g yeast
30g icing sugar
50ml milk
400g potato, cooked, unpeeled
400g butter
40g salt
700g flour
3 egg yolks

Stir the yeast and sugar into the milk in a saucepan and warm on the stove over a low heat, so that it rises. Peel and mash the cooked potatoes. Mix the potatoes, butter, salt and egg yolks together. Add the flour and milk mixture. Knead well together and let the dough rest in the fridge overnight. The next day, roll the pastry out to 1cm thick and cut out circles with a biscuit cutter. Let the scones rise for 20-30 minutes in a warm place (or for 45 minutes if the weather is cold). Bake at 180°C for 10 or 15 minutes, depending on the size of the scones.

STRUDELS

SOUR CHERRY STRUDEL (MEGGYES RÉTES)

INGREDIENTS

1kg sour cherries, stoned
150g sugar
1 tsp cinnamon
20g custard powder
1 packet of strudel pastry (6-8 sheets)
50g walnuts, coarsely chopped
sunflower oil

Add the sour cherries, sugar and cinnamon to a saucepan. Slowly simmer over a low heat. Meanwhile, mix the custard powder with 100ml of water. When the cherries begin to release their juice, add the custard powder mixture. Cook until thick. Spread a sheet of strudel pastry on a damp kitchen towel, brush with oil and repeat with another sheet. Add another sheet of pastry and spread half the cherry filling evenly on it. Sprinkle with walnuts and roll tightly. Repeat with the second half of the pastry (you will get two rolls). Place the strudel rolls on a greased baking tray and brush the tops with oil. Bake at 190°C until crisp, for about 15-20 minutes.

SOUR CHERRY AND POPPY SEED STRUDEL
(MÁKOS-MEGGYES RÉTES)

INGREDIENTS

200g ground poppy seeds
120g granulated sugar
zest of 1 orange and 1 lemon
ground cinnamon
150ml milk
300g stoned sour cherries
1 packet of strudel pastry (6-8 sheets)
oil

Bring the milk to the boil, add the cinnamon, grated orange and lemon peel and ground poppy seeds and cook together until the mixture thickens. When it is nice and mushy, mix in the sour cherries and then allow to cool.
Lay a sheet of strudel pastry on a damp tea towel, brush it with oil, lay another sheet on top, brush with oil too and follow it with a third sheet. Spread half the filling on it and roll up tightly.
Repeat with the other three sheets of pastry. Lay the strudels onto an oiled baking tray, brush the tops with oil and bake in a 190°C oven for 20 minutes until beautifully crisp and golden brown.

APPLE STRUDEL (ALMÁS RÉTES)

INGREDIENTS

1 packet of strudel pastry (6-8 sheets)
1kg green apples
200g granulated sugar
2 cinnamon sticks
1 packet of strudel pastry
100g butter
50g sliced almonds

Peel and core the apples, then cut into 2x2cm cubes. Add to a saucepan together with the sugar and cinnamon sticks, and cook over a high heat until all the liquid has evaporated. Spread a pastry sheet out on a damp tea towel, brush with melted butter, top with another sheet, brush this too and add a third. Spread over half the apple filling and roll up tightly. Repeat for the second strudel roll. Brush the tops with butter and sprinkle over the sliced almonds.
Bake in a preheated oven at 180°C for 25 minutes.

CHOCOLATE STRUDEL (CSOKOLÁDÉS RÉTES)

INGREDIENTS

100g chocolate
100g ground almonds
100g breadcrumbs
3 eggs
50ml milk
130g granulated sugar
30g plain flour
finely chopped zest of 1 orange
1 packet of strudel pastry (6-8 sheets)
20g butter

Mix the breadcrumbs, almonds, flour and orange zest together. Heat the milk with the sugar, vanilla sugar and the chocolate. Cook over a low heat until the chocolate and sugar have completely melted. Remove from the heat, add the dry ingredients and mix well together.
Separate the eggs. Mix the yolks into the filling and beat the whites with a pinch of salt until stiff before carefully folding into the totally cool mixture.
Spread out a pastry sheet, brush it with melted butter, top with the next sheet, some more butter and another sheet. Spread over the filling, roll it up, fold in the ends and lay it on a baking sheet. Repeat with the remaining pastry and filling. Brush the tops of the strudels with butter and bake for 5-6 minutes in a preheated oven at 200°C.
Then open the oven door to allow it to cool down a little, reduce the temperature to 150°C, close the door and bake for a further 10 minutes. Let it rest for at least 15 minutes before slicing.

CHESTNUT STRUDEL (GESZTENYÉS RÉTES)

INGREDIENTS
1 packet of strudel pastry (6-8 sheets)

FOR THE FILLING
250g chestnut purée
250g Philadelphia cream cheese
150g brown sugar
2 eggs
2 tbsp dark rum or rum essence
pinch of cinnamon
200g frozen stoned sour cherries

FOR GREASING THE PASTRY SHEETS
50g butter
50g chestnut honey

Beat the sugar, eggs and cream cheese for the filling together until smooth. Add the chestnut purée, rum, cinnamon and sour cherries. Melt the butter with the honey. Lay out a pastry sheet, brush with the butter and honey mixture and repeat this three times, i.e. use four pastry sheets for one strudel.
Spread half the filling onto the pastry and roll up tightly. Repeat for the second strudel. Place both into a baking tray. Brush the top of the strudels with butter and bake for 25 minutes in a preheated oven at 200°C.

HOT DESSERTS

WALNUT PANCAKE (DIÓS PALACSINTA)

INGREDIENTS

FOR THE BATTER
3 egg yolks
2 eggs
250g plain flour
200ml milk
soda water
pinch of salt
oil for frying

FOR THE FILLING
3 egg whites
150g ground walnuts
100g granulated sugar
pinch of salt

First of all, make the batter as it's good to let it rest a little before using. Mix the eggs and egg yolks with the milk and flour until smooth. Season with a pinch of salt and then add enough soda water to get a medium-thick batter.
For the filling, beat the egg whites together with a pinch of salt till stiff peaks form, adding the sugar right at the end. Fold the ground walnuts into the mixture.
Fry the pancakes in a hot, oiled pan. Spread over the filling while still hot.

NOODLE AND CURD CHEESE CAKE WITH BERRIES (VARGABÉLES)

INGREDIENTS (MAKES 10-12)

FOR THE CAKE
130g vermicelli
500g cow's milk curd cheese
150g sugar
10g vanilla sugar
4 eggs, separated
200ml sour cream
zest of 1 lemon
250g frozen strudel pastry
50g butter, melted

FOR THE SAUCE
50g sugar
100ml Tokaji aszú wine
(or other dessert wine)
1 tbsp cornflour
100g blackberries
100g blueberries
100g redcurrants

Cook the vermicelli in lightly salted water, cool, drain and set aside. Press the curd cheese through a sieve. Mix the curd cheese with 100g of sugar, vanilla sugar, the egg yolks, lemon zest and sour cream. Stir in the vermicelli. Whisk the egg whites with the remaining sugar until stiff peaks form. Fold the egg whites into the curd cheese mixture. Spread strudel sheets on a baking tray with some hanging over the edges, so it can be folded later. Drizzle with one-third of the butter and spread the curd cheese mixture on top. Fold over the overhanging pastry and place the remaining strudel sheet on top. Brush with melted butter. Bake for 40 to 45 minutes at 150°C. Leave to rest for at least half an hour before slicing. For the sauce, caramelise the sugar by adding 5ml water to it and cook until light brown, then add 200ml of water and the wine. Bring to the boil and add the cornflour dissolved in three tablespoons of cold water to thicken it. Add the fruit, bring back to the boil and then remove from the heat. Serve the sauce either hot or cold with the cake.

PANCAKES STUFFED WITH PLUM JAM AND BRANDY (SZILVALEKVÁROS PALCSINTA)

INGREDIENTS (MAKES 12)

7 eggs, whites and yolks separated
110g sugar
40g vanilla sugar
200ml milk
200ml cream
200g flour
pinch of salt
zest of 1 lemon, grated
zest of 1 orange, grated
200ml sunflower oil or butter for frying
400ml plum jam
50ml plum brandy (pálinka)

Beat the egg whites until stiff and set aside. Beat the egg yolks with the sugars until thick. Fold in the milk, cream, salt, grated lemon and orange zest, flour and egg whites. Heat the butter or oil in a crêpe pan (or a frying pan) and cook thick pancakes over a low heat. Mix the plum jam with the brandy and fill the pancakes with the mixture. Sprinkle with icing sugar to taste.

APRICOT DUMPLINGS (BARACKOS GOMBÓC)

INGREDIENTS (MAKES 20)

FOR THE DOUGH:
1kg potatoes
2 egg yolks
2 tbsp sunflower oil
150-200g flour
pinch of salt

FOR THE FILLING AND COATING:
500g apricots, halved
 or quartered, stones removed
20 sugar cubes, halved
pinch of cinnamon
150g breadcrumbs
100g butter

Cook the unpeeled potatoes. Peel them while still hot and push through a potato ricer. Mix in the egg yolks, oil and salt. Add as much flour as necessary to form a dough that can be easily rolled out. Set aside.
Meanwhile, brown the breadcrumbs in the butter in a frying pan. Set aside. Roll out the dough and cut into squares of approximately 8 centimetres. Place a piece of apricot in each square and put half a sugar cube on top. Pinch the four edges together to form a round dumpling. Cook in boiling water, then drain and toss in the breadcrumbs and cinnamon.

RICE SOUFFLÉ (RIZSFELFÚJT)

INGREDIENTS

300g rice
1l milk
100g granulated sugar
seeds from 1 vanilla pod
6 eggs
120g icing sugar
grated zest of 1 lemon

Cook the rice in 200ml water with a little salt and then gradually pour in the milk. Cook, stirring continuously, until the rice is soft. Once ready, spread out the rice on some baking paper or a tray so that it can cool down quickly. Meanwhile grate over the lemon zest and scrape out the seeds from the vanilla pod.
Beat all the eggs together with the icing sugar until light and fluffy. Stir in the cooled rice and turn the mixture into a baking tray sprinkled with breadcrumbs. Bake in a preheated oven at 160°C for 50 minutes. You can serve it in many ways – with homemade raspberry syrup, jam, preserved fruit, or even chocolate sauce.

CURD CHEESE DUMPLINGS (TÚRÓGOMBÓC)

INGREDIENTS

1 kg curd cheese
2 tbsp semolina
2 tbsp plain flour
4 tbsp oil
1 egg
2 tbsp breadcrumbs

FOR THE COATING
100g breadcrumbs
40g butter

Mix the curd cheese with the semolina, flour, oil, egg and finally the breadcrumbs. (Make sure you do it in this order!) Leave to rest for half an hour in the fridge, then, with wet hands, make uniform dumplings.
Drop the dumplings into boiling water. When they float to the top, cook for a further minute.
Melt the butter in a frying pan and fry the breadcrumbs until crisp and brown. Then turn the hot dumplings in the breadcrumb mixture. Serve with sour cream mixed with icing sugar and grated lemon zest.

HONEY- AND JAM-FILLED APPLE
(MÉZES-LEKVÁROS TÖLTÖTT ALMA)

INGREDIENTS

FOR THE PASTRY
300g flour
200g butter
100g icing sugar
1 egg yolk
1-2 tsp sour cream
grated lemon zest
1 tsp vanilla sugar
pinch of baking powder
pinch of salt

FOR THE FILLING
4 firm apples
150g coarsely ground walnuts
2-3 tbsp redcurrant or other red jam
2-3 tbsp acacia honey
1 stick of cinnamon
2 tbsp sugar
few drops of lemon juice

Mix the flour with the icing sugar, then rub together with the cold butter to form breadcrumbs. Add the pinch of salt, vanilla sugar, baking powder and grated lemon zest. Then knead together with the egg yolk and add enough sour cream to make a malleable pastry. Leave to rest in the fridge for an hour.
Peel and core the apples (make as big a hole as possible in the middle, but make sure that the apples stay in one piece). Cook them for a minute in water with some cinnamon and sugar, so that they are well infused by the water, but don't fall to pieces. Mix the walnuts with the honey and jam to make a thick mixture. Stuff the cooled apples with the mixture. Roll out the pastry thinly to form four circles of about 15cm in diameter and then place an apple in the middle of each. Make eight slits in the surrounding pastry and fold each part over onto the apple so that each partly covers the one before. Brush with a whole egg to make sure that the pastry parts stick together. If you're unsure how the process works, take a look at the next page to see how to wrap the apple in the pastry! After the apples are all wrapped, brush the outsides with a beaten egg, too. Then bake at 180°C until golden brown. You can eat them a few minutes later. But make sure you don't burn your mouth on the hot filling!

APPLE AND MERINGUE BREAD AND BUTTER PUDDING (MÁGLYARAKÁS)

INGREDIENTS

1 large brioche (500g)
1l chocolate milk
120g granulated sugar
7 eggs
250g icing sugar
1 vanilla pod
500g green apples
50g ground walnuts
100g apricot jam
30g butter

Slice the brioche into finger-thick slices and toast them a little in a 180°C oven. Bring the milk to the boil with the granulated sugar and the seeds from the vanilla pod. Pour the milk over the toasted brioche and leave to cool.
Whisk the egg yolks with 100g icing sugar until light and frothy, and then mix with the brioche. Place into a buttered baking tray and cover the top with peeled and sliced apples. Brush with apricot jam and sprinkle with walnuts.
Bake in a preheated oven at 180°C for 40 minutes.
Meanwhile start to beat half of the remaining icing sugar with the egg whites. Before they are totally stiff, add the rest of the icing sugar and continue to whisk until stiff peaks form. Spread the meringue over the brioche and bake for a further 10-12 minutes at 180°C.

CURD CHEESE DUMPLING SOUFFLÉ
(STÍRIAI METÉLT)

INGREDIENTS (SERVES 8)

500g cow's milk curd cheese
100g flour
4 eggs
pinch of salt
1l milk
200g sugar
1 vanilla pod
200ml sour cream
1 tbsp grated lemon zest
20g butter
2 tbsp breadcrumbs

Mix the curd cheese with the flour, one egg and the salt. Knead the mixture together and form finger-shaped dumplings. Heat the milk with the vanilla pod and 100g of sugar and cook the dumplings in it.
Beat the egg whites. In another bowl, beat three egg yolks with 100g of the sugar and stir in the sour cream, egg whites and lemon zest. Combine with the dumplings, stir and pour into soufflé dishes coated with butter and breadcrumbs. Bake for 20-25 minutes at 160°C.

CURD CHEESE STUFFED ROLLS
(TÚRÓVAL TÖLTÖTT ZSÖMLE)

INGREDIENTS

8 bread rolls
500g curd cheese
2 sachets of vanilla sugar
100g granulated sugar
3 egg yolks
grated zest of 1 lemon
200ml sour cream
raisins (optional)
200ml milk
500g butter

Mash the curd cheese, and mix with the vanilla sugar, sugar, egg yolks, 150ml sour cream and the grated lemon zest. Cut off the tops of the rolls, scrape out the insides, tear into small pieces and stir into the filling mixture.
Heat the milk and dip the rolls into it for a second or two, then lay them immediately onto a baking tray. Be careful not to soak them for too long or the rolls will fall apart!
Spoon the filling into the rolls, put the tops back on (dip these into the milk for a second too), brush the tops with the remaining sour cream, drizzle with melted butter and then bake in a 200°C oven for 20-25 minutes until crisp. I think they are particularly tasty when sprinkled with plenty of icing sugar. Best eaten fresh and hot from the oven!

PLUM JAM AND POPPY SEED VERMICELLI
(SZILVALEKVÁROS MÁKOS METÉLT)

INGREDIENTS

250g vermicelli
100g icing sugar
100g ground poppy seeds
150g plum jam
50g butter

FOR THE SYRUP
2 oranges
200g granulated sugar
200ml water

Cook the vermicelli in slightly salted boiling water, then strain, cool and drain thoroughly. Mix with the plum jam and then the poppy seeds mixed with icing sugar.
Add the melted butter, mix thoroughly, pour into a baking tray and then level out. Bake in a preheated oven at 160°C for 40 minutes. Meanwhile, make a thick syrup from the orange juice, grated zest, water and sugar.
Remove the vermicelli from the oven and pour over one-third of the syrup. Bake for a further 20 minutes, then pour over half the syrup, bake for a final 20 minutes and then pour over the remaining syrup. Leave to rest for 15 minutes before serving.

GOLDEN WALNUT DUMPLINGS
(ARANYGALUSKA)

INGREDIENTS

FOR THE LEAVENED DOUGH
500g plain flour
200ml milk
40g yeast
50g icing sugar
70g melted butter
5 egg yolks
pinch of salt

FOR THE CREAM
150g walnuts
150g granulated sugar
100g butter

Sift the flour and put in a warm place. Warm up the milk, add a little sugar, crumble in the yeast and leave for 10-12 minutes to prove. Then add the icing sugar to the sifted flour, as well as a pinch of salt, the egg yolks, the leavened yeast and the melted butter. Mix until smooth either by hand or with a food processor. When the first bubbles appear sprinkle over some flour, cover with a tea towel and leave in a warm place for 30 minutes to prove. Make sure you don't leave the dough somewhere that's too cool as it won't rise and that the milk is not too hot as it will kill the yeast spores.
Tear the dough into scone-sized pieces, turn in melted butter and then lay half the dumplings in the bottom of a baking tray. Sprinkle with a mixture of sugar and ground walnuts, pile on the remaining dumplings and then sprinkle these with sugar and walnuts. Bake in a preheated oven at 180°C for a good half hour.
You can also serve this with custard. Mix four egg yolks together well with eight tablespoons of sugar and a heaped tablespoon of flour, then add a teaspoon of vanilla essence. Slowly add half a litre of milk, 200ml of whipping cream and heat up.
Cook until thick, stirring continuously. Be careful, as it will continue to thicken even after you remove it from the heat. Cool before serving, although it is also delicious when lukewarm.

BAKED PLUM JAM DOUGHNUTS
(SZILVALEKVÁROS KELT FÁNK)

INGREDIENTS

500g plain flour
35g fresh yeast
250ml lukewarm milk
70g sugar
80g butter
½ tsp salt
grated zest of 1 lemon
3 egg yolks
200g plum jam
200g prunes
50ml plum brandy (pálinka)
pinch of salt

Quarter the prunes, mix with the plum brandy and leave to stand overnight. The following day, mix together with the plum jam.
Sift the flour into a bowl and crumble the yeast into 100ml lukewarm milk with a little sugar. Make a well in the centre of the flour and pour in the milk. Knead together and then sprinkle the dough with a little flour, cover with a tea towel and leave to rise in a warm place until the top cracks open a little. Then add the two egg yolks, the melted butter, the remaining sugar and milk, the lemon zest and a pinch of salt. Knead together thoroughly. Leave the dough to rise again in a warm place for about half an hour. Then roll it into small dumpling shapes. (Either quickly pinch out pieces of dough or cut out rounds with a scone cutter.) Lay the doughnuts onto a buttered baking tray and make a small depression in the middle of each with your thumb. Spoon a heaped teaspoon of the plum jam mixture into each.
Brush the doughnuts with the remaining egg yolk and bake for 25-30 minutes in a preheated oven at 200°C. Leave to cool a little before serving.

DOUGHNUTS (FÁNK)

INGREDIENTS (MAKES 15-20)

500g flour, sifted
200ml milk
40g fresh yeast
50g icing sugar, sifted
5 egg yolks
70g butter, melted
300ml sunflower oil
salt

Place the flour somewhere warm (such as on an open oven door, with the oven switched on). Warm the milk, add a pinch of salt and crumble in the yeast. Let it sit for 10 to 12 minutes to allow the yeast to rise. Mix the sugar, a pinch of salt, egg yolks and yeast mixture with the flour. Start mixing with your hands, while adding the butter. Knead until the dough is smooth and fluffy. Sprinkle with flour, cover with a kitchen towel and leave to rise in a warm place for 30 minutes. Transfer the dough to a floured surface and roll out to 2-3cm thick. Cut into 6cm circles with a biscuit cutter and sprinkle with flour. Cover again and leave to rise for a further 10 minutes. Press a hole in the centre of each doughnut. Deep-fry in medium-hot oil: cook on the first side for about three minutes and on the second for two minutes. Remove with a slotted spoon and drain on paper towels. To serve, spoon apricot jam into the centres of the doughnuts and sprinkle with icing sugar.

POPPY SEED BREAD PUDDING
(MÁKOS GUBA)

INGREDIENTS

100g ground poppy seeds
50g icing sugar
500ml milk
30g sugar
1 vanilla pod, seeds scraped out
10 bread rolls, preferably stale (or 3-4 slices of bread,
  if they are fresh, dry them in a warm oven), diced
150g mascarpone
30g butter

Mix the poppy seeds with the icing sugar. Bring the milk to the boil with the sugar and vanilla seeds. Pour it over the bread pieces. When the bread has absorbed the milk, gently toss it with the poppy seed mixture. Transfer to a baking dish, stir in the mascarpone and crumble the butter on top. Bake at 220°C for 15 minutes.

EMPEROR'S CRUMBS (CSÁSZÁRMORZSA)

INGREDIENTS

3 eggs, whites and yolks separated
100g icing sugar
100g butter
500ml milk
pinch of salt
zest of 1 lemon, grated
250g semolina
200-300 ml sparkling water
100g apricot jam

Beat the egg yolks with half the sugar and half the butter until thick. Fold in the milk, grated lemon zest, semolina and salt. In a separate bowl, beat the egg whites with the rest of the sugar until stiff. Fold in the yolk mixture, stir until smooth and add as much sparkling water as needed to make a thick batter. Heat the remaining butter in a baking pan, pour in the batter and bake at 180°C. Stir occasionally so it resembles crumbs when ready. Sprinkle with icing sugar and serve with apricot jam.

PASTA POCKETS FILLED WITH PLUM JAM
(BARÁTFÜLE)

INGREDIENTS (MAKES 20-25)

1kg potatoes
2 egg yolks
2 tbsp sunflower oil
150-200g flour
200g plum jam
150g breadcrumbs
100g butter
pinch of salt

Cook the unpeeled potatoes. Peel and then press them through a potato ricer while still hot. Stir in the egg yolks, oil, salt and enough flour to make the dough easy to roll out. Let it cool. Meanwhile, brown the breadcrumbs in the butter in a frying pan. Roll out the dough and cut into squares of approximately 8cm. Place a spoonful of jam into each square then fold in half and press together. Cook in boiling water, drain, and toss in the breadcrumbs.

SOUR CHERRY PURSES
(MEGGYES ERSZÉNY)

INGREDIENTS

FOR THE BUTTER PASTRY
550g plain flour
500g butter
2 eggs
1 tbsp vinegar
pinch of salt

FOR THE FILLING
1kg sour cherries
1 sachet custard powder
200g sugar
100ml cold water
2 egg yolks

Rub together 50g butter with 50g flour, shape into a rectangle and put into the fridge. While it is chilling, knead together the remaining flour and butter, a pinch of salt and the vinegar to form a pastry. Leave to rest for 30 minutes on a floured board covered with a tea towel. Roll out to a finger-thick and place the chilled butter in the centre. Fold in the pastry from all four sides and roll it out again to a finger thick rectangular shape. Then roll it out again both in a single and a double pleat. Repeat this several times.
Leave to rest in a cool place for 20 minutes between each folding and rolling. For the single pleat, mentally divide the rectangular pastry into three, fold one side one-third in, then fold over the remaining third and then roll out lengthwise to form a rectangle again. For the double pleat, mentally divide the rectangular pastry into two and fold the two edges into the middle, then fold the whole thing into the middle and roll out lengthwise. Keep the finished butter pastry in the fridge; always work quickly with it, so the butter it contains does not have time to melt.
Roll out the pastry thinly and cut into 5x10cm rectangles. Spoon the filling into the centre of the pastry pieces and fold over one of the empty sides of the pastry. Brush with egg yolk and then fold over the other side of the pastry – they should stick together now.
Then turn over the pastry so that the joined side is facing down and, using a sharp knife, cut slashes into the pastry top. Brush with the other egg yolk and bake in a 190°C oven for 20-25 minutes.

PRUNE AND MARZIPAN FRITTERS
(LAKATOSINAS)

INGREDIENTS

40 stoned prunes
200ml rum
200g marzipan
3 tbsp icing sugar
1 level tsp cinnamon
oil for frying

FOR THE PANCAKE BATTER
2 eggs
80g flour
100ml milk
pinch of salt
water

First of all prepare the pancake batter, because it's not a bad idea to let it rest a little. Beat the eggs together with the flour, milk and salt, and then add enough water to get a thick pancake batter. Set aside to rest.

Heat the rum a little and then soak the prunes in it for half an hour. Once they have plumped up, remove them from the rum (you can drink the rest) and dry them with a paper towel.

Stuff the middle of each prune with a little marzipan, then dip the plums into the pancake batter and fry in hot oil. Drain and sprinkle with cinnamon and icing sugar while still hot.

JAM-FILLED CRESCENT ROLL FRITTERS
(LEKVÁROS KIFLI)

INGREDIENTS

8 crescent rolls (2-3 days old)
200ml milk
1 sachet of vanilla sugar
50g granulated sugar
apricot jam
vegetable oil for frying

FOR THE BATTER
2 eggs
80g flour
100ml milk
pinch of salt
water

First prepare the batter: beat the egg with the flour, milk and salt, and then add enough water to obtain a good thick pancake batter. Bring the milk to the boil with the sugar and vanilla sugar.
Cut the crescent rolls in half (not like you're making a sandwich, but crosswise) and push your finger right inside the roll. Spoon a couple of teaspoons of the vanilla milk into each roll and then a teaspoon of jam.
Coat the rolls in the pancake batter and fry in hot oil. Serve sprinkled with sugar and cinnamon.

CHIMNEY CAKE (KÜRTŐS KALÁCS)

INGREDIENTS:

Same dough as for the 'golden' dumplings (see page 92.)

FOR THE CINNAMON VARIANT:
120g granulated sugar, 1 tsp ground cinnamon
FOR THE WALNUT VARIANT:
100g granulated sugar, 50g ground walnuts

Roll out the dough thinly and cut into 1cm-wide strips. If you don't have any special 'chimney cake' rods, use a rolling pin instead. Lightly coat the rolling pin with oil and tightly wind the dough strips around it. Rub it with wet hands and then sprinkle over the walnut or cinnamon sugar. Wrap the handle with aluminium foil to prevent it from burning. Then bake to golden brown over hot coals, turning constantly.

GUNDEL PANCAKE (GUNDEL PALACSINTA)

INGREDIENTS:

FOR THE PANCAKE
3 egg yolks
2 eggs
250g flour
200ml milk
soda water
pinch of salt

FOR THE FILLING
150g ground walnuts
80g granulated sugar
200ml water
grated zest and juice of 1 orange

FOR THE SAUCE
100g plain chocolate
100ml cream
30ml dark rum

First of all prepare the batter. Then leave it to rest for a little before using as this will improve it.
Beat the eggs and the egg yolks together with the milk and flour until smooth. Add a pinch of salt to the batter and then enough soda water to form a medium-thick batter.
Bring the water, sugar and orange for the sauce to the boil. Sprinkle in the walnuts and cook for 2-3 minutes.
Heat the ingredients for the sauce in a bain-marie to a maximum of 70°C.
Fry thin pancakes from the batter in a hot, oiled frying pan. Spread them with the filling while still hot. Fold them into triangles and drizzle with the rum and chocolate sauce.

BUNS WITH COCOA, CINNAMON, PLUM JAM OR WALNUTS (KAKAÓS CSIGA)

INGREDIENTS (MAKES 15 PIECES)

500 g puff pastry

FOR THE FILLING, ONE OF THE FOLLOWING:
thick homemade plum jam
cinnamon mixed with sugar
ground walnuts mixed with icing sugar,
or good quality cocoa powder
1 egg yolk, lightly beaten

Roll out the puff pastry dough to 2mm thick and 20cm wide. Brush with whichever filling you choose and tightly roll up the dough. Lay the pieces on a greased and floured baking tray. Cut slices that are approximately 5mm thick and, with your hands, press each piece lightly. Brush with the egg yolk. Bake in an oven at 170°C until ready (15-20 minutes).

MISCELLANEOUS

PLUM TART (SZILVÁS LEPÉNY)

INGREDIENTS

FOR THE PASTRY
300g plain flour
200g butter
100g icing sugar
1 egg yolk
1-2 tsp sour cream
grated lemon zest
1 tsp vanilla sugar
pinch of baking powder
pinch of salt

FOR THE FILLING
600g plums
150g brown sugar
1 tsp ground cinnamon
1 handful of chopped walnuts
3 tbsp plum jam
1 egg yolk

Mix the flour together with the icing sugar and then rub in the cold butter. Add a pinch of salt, the vanilla sugar, baking powder and grated lemon zest. Then knead together with the egg yolk and add enough sour cream to form a kneadable dough. Leave to rest in the fridge for an hour.
Halve the plums, remove the stones and then cut into quarters. Simmer the plum jam together with the sugar and cinnamon, then add the plums and bring to the boil.
Line a 25cm flan tin with two-thirds of the pastry. Bake blind in an oven preheated to 150°C for 10-15 minutes until golden brown. Then leave to cool. Now spoon in the filling. (If it's is too runny, you can mix in a couple of tablespoons of breadcrumbs.) Sprinkle with the coarsely chopped walnuts. Roll out the remaining pastry, and cut into rectangles and then into strips.
Lay the pastry strips over the filling in a lattice pattern. Brush with the egg yolk and bake for 30-35 minutes in an oven preheated to 170°C.

RASPBERRY AND CREAM SPONGE ROLL
(MÁLNÁS-HABOS PISKÓTATEKERCS)

INGREDIENTS

FOR THE CREAM
500ml double cream
300g raspberries
grated zest of 1 orange
10ml orange liqueur (triple sec)
   or orange essence
10g vanilla sugar
40g granulated sugar
200g whipped cream stabiliser

FOR THE SPONGE CAKE
4 eggs
80g plain flour
80g granulated sugar
2 tbsp water
pinch of salt

Beat the egg yolks together with the sugar and then gradually mix in the flour, too. Whisk the egg whites until stiff peaks form and then gently fold into the mixture together with the water. Spread the mixture thinly into a large, flat baking tray lined with greaseproof paper and bake in a preheated oven at 180°C until golden brown.
Turn out the sponge and remove the paper while still hot. Roll up the sponge tightly and wrap back into the paper, or alternatively in a tea towel if you were unable to remove the paper in one piece. It's important to roll the sponge cake tightly while hot since if you do this when cold, the sponge will break up. Make the filling while the sponge is cooling down. Beat the cream with the cream stabiliser and sugar until stiff. Set aside about six tablespoons to decorate the outside of the cake and flavour the rest with the orange liqueur, orange zest and vanilla sugar. Mix in the raspberries and spread the sponge with the mixture. Roll up the whole thing gently, then spread the outside with the remaining cream and chill in the fridge for at least 5-6 hours. Serve cut into thick slices.

SEMOLINA CREAM WITH PRUNES
(ASZALT SZILVÁS DARAPUDING)

INGREDIENTS

1l milk
180g semolina
200g sugar
1 vanilla pod
500g prunes
pinch of salt
200ml cream
½ tsp cinnamon

Cut the prunes into small pieces and mix with the cinnamon. Bring the milk to the boil with the seeds scraped from the vanilla pod, and add the semolina, a pinch of salt and half the sugar. Simmer over a low heat, stirring constantly.
Transfer the semolina into another dish, mix in the prunes and wait for it to cool a little. Whip the cream with the remaining sugar until thick and fold gently into the semolina. Pour into glasses or a meatloaf tin and chill for 2-3 hours in the fridge.
Serve drizzled with melted plum jam or caramel.

QUINCE CHEESE (BIRSALMASAJT)

INGREDIENTS

2kg quinces
1.65kg granulated sugar
2 lemons
300ml water

I got his recipe from my dearest grandma; she was always making quince cheese. It's very easy to make: peel and slice the quinces, and make some syrup from the sugar, water and lemon juice.
Add the quinces, cover and cook until tender, stirring occasionally. Pass through a fine sieve – you could also add some walnuts here, if you like – and cook for a further 17 minutes. Why 17 minutes? I don't know, but let's leave it like this out of respect for my grandma! Then pour into moulds and leave in a cool place to set before slicing.

FLOATING ISLANDS (MADÁRTEJ)

INGREDIENTS

1500ml semi-skimmed milk
1 vanilla pod
9 tbsp sugar
6 eggs
1 tsp custard powder
grated zest of half a lemon

Set aside 50ml of the milk, you will need this later. Add the vanilla pod to the rest of the milk along with seven tablespoons of sugar and then bring to the boil.
Beat two tablespoons of sugar together with the egg whites until they form stiff peaks. Use a tablespoon to scoop out good-sized balls from the meringue and place them in the simmering milk. Cook them for half a minute on each side and then remove.
Mix the 50ml of milk you set aside earlier with the egg yolks, custard powder and lemon zest. Add this to the vanilla milk and cook the whole mixture until it thickens nicely.
Serve everyone some of the custard and top with some meringue balls.

CREAM SLICES (VAJAS KRÉMES)

INGREDIENTS

FOR THE PASTRY
320g plain flour
60g butter
20g lard or vegetable fat
100g icing sugar
½ sachet of baking powder
2 eggs

FOR THE CREAM
2 sachets of custard powder
1l full fat milk
250g butter
200g icing sugar
1 sachet of vanilla sugar

Mix the pastry ingredients together, then divide the pastry into three equal parts and roll each out thinly. Preheat the oven to 180°C, place onto a baking sheet and bake for 10 minutes.

To make the cream, mix the custard powder into 300ml of cold milk. Bring the remaining milk to the boil and gradually add the custard powder and milk mixture, stirring constantly. Cook until thick and set to one side. Beat the butter with the icing sugar and the vanilla sugar until creamy, and then mix thoroughly with the cooled custard.

Spread one pastry sheet with the cream, then add another sheet and some more cream and finally top with the third layer. Chill for 2-3 hours. It's easier to slice when cold.

FROSTED SLICES (ZÚZMARA SZELET)

INGREDIENTS

FOR THE CAKE
4 eggs
200g icing sugar
140g plain flour
100g melted butter
1 sachet of baking powder
pinch of salt

FOR THE CREAM
200ml milk
3 heaped tbsp semolina
200g butter
200g granulated sugar
1 vanilla pod
apricot jam

Separate the eggs. Beat the egg whites with a pinch of salt until stiff peaks form. Then add the egg yolks one by one and gradually mix in the icing sugar. Add the baking powder mixed with flour, stirring constantly, and finally the melted butter.
Pour the batter into a buttered and floured baking tin and bake in a preheated oven at 170°C for 20 minutes. Once the cake has cooled down, cut in half crosswise.
To make the cream, heat the milk with the seeds from the vanilla pod. Sprinkle in the semolina, stirring constantly, and cook until thick. Beat the butter and cream to a thick cream and then mix together with the cooled semolina.
Chill the cream slightly in the fridge. Spread the base sponge cake sheet with apricot jam, followed by the semolina cream, cover with the other sponge cake sheet and sprinkle with icing sugar.

ZSERBÓ SLICE (ZSERBÓ)

INGREDIENTS

FOR THE DOUGH
400g plain flour
250g butter
50g yeast
200ml sour cream

FOR THE FILLING
130g granulated sugar
130g coarsely ground walnuts
1 sachet vanilla sugar
grated zest of 1 lemon
apricot jam

FOR THE CHOCOLATE GLAZE
100g sugar
100g butter
2 tbsp cocoa
2 tbsp milk

Knead the ingredients for the cake together, then wrap in foil and put in the fridge overnight. The following day, divide into four parts and roll out into thin baking-tray sized sheets. Mix the sugar with the walnuts and lemon zest to make the filling.
Lay the first sheet of pastry into the bottom of the baking tray, spread with jam and sprinkle over the sugar and walnuts. Put another sheet of pastry on top, with some more jam, followed by walnuts. Repeat the whole process until the ingredients run out (finishing with a sheet of pastry on the top).
Bake in a medium oven at about 150-160°C. Leave to cool in the baking tray and then turn out onto a board. Mix together the ingredients for the chocolate glaze, bring to the boil and then leave to cool for 15 minutes before coating the Zserbó with it.
Leave to cool before serving.

POPPY SEED CUP CAKE (BÖGRÉS MÁKOS)

INGREDIENTS

2 eggs
100g butter
1 cup sugar
1 cup plain flour
1 cup ground poppy seeds
1 cup milk
1 sachet of baking powder
1 sachet of vanilla sugar
1 tsp vanilla
1 tbsp honey

Beat the butter and sugar together until thick and creamy, then mix in the eggs, followed by the milk, then the baking powder and flour, and finally the poppy seeds. Flavour with cinnamon and honey, and pour into a buttered and floured baking tray.
Cook in a preheated oven at 170°C for 35-40 minutes. Leave the cake to cool a little, turn it out, cut in half, spread the bottom layer with apricot jam and put the top layer back. Dust with icing sugar before serving.

HONEY CREAM SLICES (MÉZES KRÉMES)

INGREDIENTS

FOR THE PASTRY
50g butter
400g flour
150g granulated sugar
1 egg
½ tsp bicarbonate of soda
3-4 tbsp milk
60g honey

FOR THE FILLING
200g butter
200g granulated sugar
zest of 1 lemon
300ml milk
60g semolina
150g apricot jam

First make the pastry by beating the honey, sugar, butter and egg together until smooth. Place the mixing bowl in a bain-marie and cook until thick, stirring constantly. Remove from the heat, cool until lukewarm and then fold in the flour together with the bicarbonate of soda.

Knead the dough, divide into four equal parts and put in the fridge for 30 minutes. Remove from the fridge and then roll each part out thinly. Lay each sheet on a baking tray and bake for 8-10 minutes in a preheated oven at 180°C.

Beat the butter and sugar until thick and creamy. Bring the milk to the boil, add the semolina and cook for a few minutes, stirring constantly. Remove from the heat, allow to cool, add the butter and sugar mixture and the lemon zest, and whisk together until smooth with an electric whisk.

Spread the first sheet of pastry thinly with jam and one-third of the cream, and place the next sheet on top. Repeat with more jam, cream, another pastry sheet, jam, cream and the final pastry sheet. Gently press the cake together, put it into the fridge and allow to soften for at least 4-5 hours. It's best to chill for at least half a day, but preferably a whole day.

NON PLUS ULTRA (NON PLUS ULTRA)

INGREDIENTS

FOR THE BISCUITS
200g plain flour
200g butter
50g vanilla sugar
2 egg yolks

FOR THE ICING
200g icing sugar
2 egg whites
a couple of drops of lemon juice

FOR THE FILLING
150g apricot jam

Mix together the ingredients for the biscuits and leave to rest for 30 minutes in the fridge. Remove from the fridge, roll out thinly, cut out 3-4cm diameter biscuits and lay on a baking sheet.
Beat the egg whites until thick and frothy, and then add the sugar and lemon juice. Make sure it's not too stiff, but rather a creamy mousse.
Spoon the egg white glaze on top of the biscuits and bake for 10-15 minutes at 160°C. Once the biscuits have cooled down, stick them together in pairs and they are ready.

APPLE AND CREAM SLICE
(ALMÁS KRÉMES)

INGREDIENTS (SERVES 10-12)

FOR THE PASTRY
100g butter
100g sugar
6g baking powder
300g flour
1 egg
50ml milk

FOR THE CREAM
400ml milk
100g sugar
100ml whipping cream
100g butter, chopped
20g custard powder
20g icing sugar

FOR THE FILLING
1.5 kg apples, peeled and diced or grated
150g sugar
1 tsp cinnamon

For the pastry, cream the sugar and butter together until light and fluffy. Add the milk, egg and baking powder mixed with the flour. Stir with a wooden spoon until smooth. Divide the pastry into three equal parts and roll out thinly. Bake on separate baking trays at 180°C. Meanwhile, stew the apples with the sugar and cinnamon until light brown. Bring 300ml of the milk and the sugar to the boil. Dissolve the custard powder in the remaining milk and then pour it into the boiling milk, stirring continuously until thick. Stir the butter into the hot milk mixture. Whip the cream with the icing sugar until stiff. When the custard is cool, fold in the whipped cream.
To assemble, spread the apple mixture on a sheet of pastry, place another pastry sheet on top, spread the cream mixture over it and finally cover with the last pastry sheet. Sprinkle with icing sugar and leave to rest for 3-4 hours to cool before serving.

PEAR CAKE WITH ALMONDS
KÖRTÉS MANDULÁS PITE

INGREDIENTS (MAKES 12 SLICES)

FOR THE PASTRY
300g flour
100g icing sugar
200g cold butter
pinch of salt
5g vanilla sugar
2.5g baking powder
1 tsp grated lemon zest
1 egg yolk
1-2 tbsp sour cream

FOR THE FILLING
1 cinnamon stick
2-3 cloves
100g sugar
juice of 1 lemon
1kg pears,
 peeled and cut into wedges
2 tbsp apricot jam
50g almonds, sliced or
 coarsely ground

Cook the pears in a saucepan with water, cinnamon, cloves, sugar and lemon juice, until they are semi-tender. Remove from the liquid (which, when cool, makes a nice drink). Set aside.
For the dough, mix the flour with the icing sugar and crumble in the butter. Add the salt, vanilla sugar, baking powder and grated lemon zest. Knead in the egg yolk. Add the sour cream, if needed, to make the pastry easier to roll out. Leave to rest for an hour in the fridge. Thinly roll out the pastry. Line the bottom of a round baking tin with half the pastry. Bake at 180°C for 10 minutes. Let it cool a little and brush with apricot jam, sprinkle with almonds, arrange the pear wedges on top and sprinkle with vanilla sugar. Grate the remaining pastry over the top of the pears. Bake until light brown at 180°C for 50-60 minutes. Serve warm with vanilla ice cream.

SOMLÓ TRIFLE (SOMLÓI GALUSKA)

INGREDIENTS

FOR THE CAKE:
12 eggs
12 tbsp flour
pinch of salt
1 tbsp cocoa powder
80g ground walnuts
1 sachet of baking powder

FOR THE CUSTARD:
6 egg whites
300ml milk
300ml cream
120g granulated sugar
vanilla essence

FOR DRIZZLING:
juice and grated zest of 2 oranges
50g raisins
100g granulated sugar
chocolate sauce
whipped cream

Beat the egg yolks and sugar together until creamy, then add the stiffly beaten egg white and a pinch of salt. Then gradually fold in the flour mixed with the baking powder, too. Divide the mixture into three. Leave the first plain, and mix the cocoa powder into the second and the ground walnuts into the third.
Spread the mixture into three lined baking trays and bake at 180°C for 12 minutes.
Beat the egg yolks together with the sugar, cream and finally the milk. Then cook in a bain-marie until thick. Flavour with half a teaspoon of vanilla essence.
Lay the walnut sponge cake into a deep bowl and sprinkle over some raisins and orange juice and zest. Spread over one-third of the custard, then lay in the plain sponge, sprinkle over more raisins and orange juice and the second third of the custard. Cover with the chocolate sponge, then with more orange juice and custard. Sprinkle the top with cocoa powder and leave to chill for at least 12 hours in the fridge. To serve, drizzle over some chocolate sauce and pipe some cream on top.

LINZER JAM SANDWICH BISCUITS
(LINZERKARIKA)

INGREDIENTS
300g flour
200g butter
100g icing sugar
1 egg yolk
1-2 tsp sour cream
grated lemon zest
pinch of salt
homemade apricot jam
icing sugar

Mix the flour and the icing sugar, and then rub in the cold butter. Add a pinch of salt, the vanilla sugar and the grated lemon zest. Then knead in the egg yolk and add enough sour cream to get a malleable pastry. Leave to rest for at least an hour in the fridge before using. Roll the pastry out thinly and cut out 4-5cm diameter circles with a wavy edged biscuit cutter, then cut out 1cm circles from the middles of half of the circles. Place on a lined baking tray and bake for 12-15 minutes.
When cooled to lukewarm, spread the biscuits with no holes with jam and stick the tops on. Sprinkle with icing sugar and leave to stand for at least half a day, although you will be really tempted to eat them before that!

FLÓDNI JEWISH CAKE (FLÓDNI)

INGREDIENTS:

FOR THE PASTRY:
550g flour
100g icing sugar
250g butter
2 egg yolks
1 egg for glazing
approx. 100ml white wine
pinch of salt

Knead the ingredients for the pastry together, then wrap in cling film and leave to rest for a day in the fridge.

FOR THE WALNUT FILLING:
200g ground walnuts
500g coarsely chopped walnuts
100ml white wine
140g sugar
30g raisins
grated zest and juice of 1 orange
pinch of salt

Bring all the ingredients except the walnuts to the boil. Then sprinkle in the nuts and cook for a further 2-3 minutes. Set to one side and leave to cool.

FOR THE POPPY SEED FILLING:
250g ground poppy seeds
grated zest and juice of 1 orange
80g sugar
100ml water
pinch of salt

Bring all the ingredients except the poppy seeds to the boil. Then add the poppy seeds and cook for a further 1-2 minutes. Set to one side and leave to cool.

FOR THE APPLE FILLING:
1kg apples, peeled and sliced
2 sticks of cinnamon
150g sugar

Stew the apples together with the sugar and cinnamon sticks until all the liquid has evaporated.

Cut the pastry into four equal parts. Roll out each part as you need it so that the pastry does not dry out. Butter a baking tray and then smooth in the first sheet of pastry. Then spread over the poppy seed filling, followed by another sheet of pastry. Then add the walnut filling and a further sheet of pastry. Spread the apple filling over the last sheet of pastry and then cover with the final sheet of pastry. Brush with beaten egg, prick with a fork and bake at 170°C for 90 minutes.

COCONUT BALLS (KÓKUSZGOLYÓ)

INGREDIENTS (MAKES 15-20 PIECES)

350g crushed sweet or butter biscuits
30g cocoa powder
100g icing sugar
100g butter
100-200ml sour cherry juice
100g desiccated coconut for sprinkling

Mix the crushed biscuits and the icing sugar together. Add the butter and enough sour cherry juice to form an easily kneadable dough. Leave to rest for half an hour in the fridge, then shape into small balls and turn them in the desiccated coconut.

SOUR CHERRY PIE (MEGGYES PITE)

INGREDIENTS

FOR THE DOUGH
300g flour
200g butter
100g icing sugar
1 egg yolk
1-2 tsp sour cream
grated lemon zest
pinch of salt

FOR THE FILLING
500g fresh or frozen stoned sour cherries, drained
120g granulated sugar
50g ground walnuts
1 tbsp ground cinnamon

Mix the flour and icing sugar together and then rub in the cold butter. Add a pinch of salt, the vanilla sugar and the grated lemon zest. Finally knead in the egg yolk and add enough sour cream to get a malleable pastry. Leave to rest in the fridge for an hour prior to use. Line a low-rimmed 25cm cake tin with two-thirds of the pastry. Bake at 180°C for 10-15 minutes until golden brown and then leave to cool. Mix the ingredients for the filling together and spread over the cooked pastry base. Grate the remaining pastry over the top and bake at 180°C for 30 minutes.

WALNUT CRESCENTS (DIÓS KIFLI)

INGREDIENTS

140g butter
70g icing sugar
70g ground walnuts
170g plain flour
grated zest of 1 lemon
vanilla sugar

These are very simple yet delicious biscuits, which in my experience, everyone really loves. They are not difficult to make either. Whip the butter and then mix in the other ingredients. Knead together well, roll into long fingers, cut into pieces and then shape into small crescents. Place on a lined or well buttered baking sheet and bake at 150-160°C until golden brown. Turn in the vanilla sugar while still hot so they are infused with a lovely vanilla flavour.

FRIED CURD CHEESE DOUGHNUT
(SÜLT TÚRÓFÁNK)

INGREDIENTS

FOR THE DOUGH
500g curd cheese
100g icing sugar
grated zest of 1 lemon
grated zest of 1 lime
4 eggs
seeds from 1 vanilla pod
100g plain flour
some breadcrumbs
pinch of salt
oil for frying

FOR THE SAUCE
250g raspberries
50g granulated sugar

Thoroughly mix the curd cheese with the lemon and lime zest, egg yolks, vanilla seeds and flour. Finally, add the stiffly beaten egg whites and enough breadcrumbs to form a dense dough.
Let the dough rest for 10 minutes. Using a spoon, make large dumplings or scone shapes from the dough and fry in medium-hot oil. Fry until golden brown on both sides.
Stew the raspberries and then pass through a fine sieve. Serve the doughnuts sprinkled with sugar and the sauce, either hot or warm.

CHESTNUT PURÉE (GESZTENYEPÜRÉ)

INGREDIENTS

250g chestnut purée
300ml double cream
100g icing sugar
2 tbsp dark rum

Mix the chestnut purée together with the rum and icing sugar, and then refrigerate. Beat the cream until thick. To serve, spoon a layer of whipped cream into the bottom of a small bowl. Pass the chestnut purée though a potato ricer or grate and layer it on top of the cream.
You can serve it with sour cherries cooked in a balsamic vinegar syrup, or you could grate some chocolate onto the top, or you could even liven it up with a couple of blackberries or blueberries.

CURD CHEESE PARCELS (TÚRÓS BATYU)

INGREDIENTS

FOR THE DOUGH
500g plain flour
35g fresh yeast
250ml lukewarm milk
70g sugar
80g butter
½ tsp salt
grated zest of 1 lemon
3 egg yolks

FOR THE FILLING
1kg curd cheese
100ml sour cream
grated zest of 1 lemon
220g icing sugar
30g vanilla sugar

Sift the flour into a bowl and crumble the yeast into 100ml lukewarm milk with a little sugar. Make a well in the centre of the flour and pour in the milk. Knead together and then sprinkle the dough with a little flour, cover with a tea towel and leave to rise in a warm place until the top cracks open a little. Then add the two egg yolks, the melted butter, the remaining sugar and milk, the lemon zest and a pinch of salt. Knead together thoroughly. Leave the dough to rise again in a warm place for about half an hour.
Meanwhile mix the filling ingredients together in a food processor.
Roll out the dough thinly and cut out 15x15cm rectangles. Place a large spoonful of the curd cheese mixture in the middle of each and pinch the four corners of the dough in together. Lay them into a baking tray about 2-3cm from each other. Leave to rise for 20 minutes and then bake in a preheated oven at 180°C for 30-35 minutes. Served sprinkled with icing sugar.

SWEET TWISTED FRITTERS (CSÖRÖGE FÁNK)

INGREDIENTS

80g butter
350g flour
80g sugar
1 sachet of vanilla sugar
5 egg yolks
2tbsp sour cream
1tbsp rum
pinch of salt
sunflower oil for frying

Melt the butter. Sift the flour into a deep bowl, mix in the sugar, vanilla sugar and a pinch of salt, add the egg yolks, melted butter, 1 tbsp sour cream and rum, and mix together thoroughly. Leave covered to rest in a cool place for half an hour.
Roll out the dough on a floured board until about 3mm thick, cut out squares of about 8-10cm in length using a ravioli cutter and make 0.5cm cuts 1cm in from each corner. Twist in the corners using these, working around the dough each time.
Heat plenty of oil in a large pan, fry the fritters in small quantities on both sides and drain on kitchen paper. Arrange on a large dish and serve hot, sprinkled with the vanilla sugar.

DILL AND CURD CHEESE PIE
(KAPROS-TÚRÓS LEPÉNY)

INGREDIENTS

FOR THE DOUGH
300g flour
200g butter
100g icing sugar
1 egg yolk
1-2 tsp sour cream
grated lemon zest
pinch of salt

FOR THE FILLING
500g crumbled cow's curd cheese
5 egg whites
100ml sour cream
160g icing sugar
80g semolina
2 bunches of finely chopped dill
1 egg yolk for glazing

Mix the flour with the icing sugar and then rub in the cold butter. Add a pinch of salt, the vanilla sugar and grated lemon zest. Knead together with the egg yolk and add enough sour cream to get a malleable dough. Leave to rest for an hour in the fridge before using.
Roll out half the dough, lay in a baking tray and bake at 180°C for 10–15 minutes until golden brown. Leave to cool.
Meanwhile, mix the ingredients for the filling together and spread over the dough. Roll out the rest of the dough, place on top of the curd cheese filling and prick with a fork to allow any steam to escape. Brush with the egg yolk mixed with a little water and bake at 180°C until golden brown.

CHOCOLATE AND WALNUT CAKE
(HUNGÁRIA SZELET)

INGREDIENTS

FOR THE CAKE
6 eggs
300g granulated sugar
10 tbsp cold water
100g ground walnuts
1 sachet of baking powder
200g plain flour

FOR THE GLAZE
14 tbsp granulated sugar
7 tbsp cocoa powder
6 tbsp water
60g butter

FOR THE CREAM
2 egg yolks
2 tbsp plain flour
250ml milk
200g butter
200g icing sugar
100g ground walnuts

To make the cake, beat the egg yolks with 200g sugar until white and creamy. Add the water and continue to whisk, and then fold in the walnuts, flour and baking powder. Beat the egg whites until stiff peaks form. Sprinkle in the remaining sugar at the end and continue to beat until firm. Fold the meringue into the water, flour and nut mixture. Then smooth the mixture into a buttered, floured baking tray (approx. 30x35cm). Bake in a preheated oven at 180°C for 20-22 minutes.

For the cream, whisk the egg yolks with the flour and water until smooth. Cook the mixture into a thick cream, stirring continuously, then leave to cool. Beat the butter and icing sugar together until smooth, then add the walnuts and the cooled cream one spoon at a time.

Cut the cake in half horizontally. Spread one half with some cream, place the other half on top and spread with the remaining cream. Place the ingredients for the glaze into a small saucepan and cook together for a few minutes until you have a smooth cream. Leave to cool a little and then spread over the cake. Once the cream has set, slice the cake with a knife dipped in hot water.

PLAITED BRIOCHE (FOSZLÓS KALÁCS)

INGREDIENTS

300ml milk
2 tbsp sugar
30g fresh yeast
1 measuring spoon salt
500g flour
1 egg white
100g lard or vegetable fat

Heat the milk until lukewarm, add the sugar and allow it to melt, crumble in the yeast and leave to prove in a warm place.
Put the sifted, lukewarm flour into a mixing bowl, add the salt, egg white, the yeast and the milk mixture. Combine it well together by hand and leave to rise in a warm place covered with a tea towel for 40 minutes. Turn the dough out onto a floured board and roll out to 1cm thick. Spread over the lard or vegetable fat, previously beaten until creamy, roll it up like a Swiss roll and leave to rest for 10 minutes. Then roll the dough in such a way that you twist the two ends in opposite directions until the dough roll is twice as long. Plait it into a brioche and then leave it to rest in a greased baking tin for 20 minutes. Place into an oven preheated to 190°C. Meanwhile dissolve two tablespoons of sugar in two tablespoons of boiling water. After 15 minutes of baking, when the brioche has started to brown, brush with half the sugar and water mixture. Bake for a further 15-20 minutes, remove from the oven and brush with the remaining sugar syrup. Leave to rest for half an hour before enjoying.

NOTES

NOTES

NOTES

NOTES

NOTES